WORK~~BOOK~~

For

Big Heart Little Stove

Bringing Home Meals
& Moments from The
Lost Kitchen

Miller Publishing

THIS BOOK BELONGS TO

Copyright © 2023 by Miller Publishing

All rights reserved. No part of this book may be reproduced or transmitted in any form or by any means, electronic or mechanical, including photocopying, recording, or by any information storage and retrieval system, without written permission from the author or publisher, except for the inclusion of brief quotations in a review.

DISCLAIMER

This is an UNOFFICIAL workbook and not the original book. This workbook is not affiliated, authorized, approved, or licensed by the subject book's author or publisher. This workbook is meant to be a companion to the original book

USING YOUR WORKBOOK AS A COMPANION

Welcome to your big heart little stove Recipe Workbook. This space is designed to complement and enrich your culinary journey, ensuring that you have the freedom to customize it according to your tastes and preferences.

Instead of listing out every ingredient or recipe, this workbook is here to serve as your cooking companion. It's your canvas to create, adapt, and organize the culinary world as you see fit.

Why Use Your Workbook This Way?

1. Personalization:Your original recipe books, family traditions, and online sources are rich with culinary inspiration. Use your workbook to adapt and personalize these recipes according to your preferences.

2. Adaptation:Don't feel constrained by lists or instructions. Instead, use the space to jot down your own creative ideas, variations, and flavor experiments.

3. Organization:Use the categories and sections within this workbook to keep your culinary resources and notes in one place. Whether it's a note about a cherished family recipe or cooking technique you've learned, this is the space to keep them organized.

4. Reflection: Make notes about your experiences, what worked and what didn't. Reflect on your culinary journey and how your skills and tastes evolve over time.

5. Inspiration: This workbook is your source of inspiration. Refer back to it when you want to brainstorm ideas or enhance your favorite dishes.

By leaving out specific lists and encouraging you to consult your original sources, we're inviting you to make this workbook truly your own. Every mark you make, every note you jot down, and every idea you record here is a reflection of your unique culinary story.

So, as you embark on your cooking adventures, let your workbook be your creative haven, a place to inspire your culinary curiosity, and your trusted companion in the world of flavors. Let's dive into your culinary story and make it uniquely yours. Happy cooking!

HAPPY COOKING

YOUR CULINARY ADVE[NTURE] BEGINS

Welcome to your very own Recipe Journal! Th[is] collection of recipes; it's your personal culinary jour[ney] space to explore, experiment, and savor the art of cooking.

Whether you're a seasoned chef or a kitchen novice, this journal is your canvas to express your creativity, your laboratory to experiment with tastes, and your time capsule to capture cherished culinary memories.

Why a Recipe Journal?

1. Organization: No more scrambling through scattered recipe notes. Your journal is your organized sanctuary, where recipes, conversions, and tips all find thei[r]

2.Creativity:Use this space to dream up your own culinar[y] creations. Who knows, you might discover the next family favorite.

3. Progress Tracking:Watch yourself evolve from hesitan[t] cook to confident chef. Document your journey with each dish you prepare .

Memories: Capture the laughter, the shared meals, and the moments that unfold around your dining table. Your journal is a keeper of stories as much as it is a keeper of recipes.

Inspiration: As you explore recipes from around the world and create your variations, your journal becomes a source of inspiration for future meals and gatherings.

In this journal, you'll find spaces to fill in your most-loved recipes, ingredient conversions, and personal notes. It's a reflection of your unique culinary identity, so don't hesitate to add your own twists, ideas, and anecdotes to every page.

So, fasten your apron, preheat the oven, and let's embark on a culinary adventure like no other. Your Recipe Journal is your trusted companion, and every page is a fresh canvas for your culinary masterpieces.

Now, let's flip the page and start your culinary story. Happy cooking!

CONVERSION CHART

Creating a conversion chart is a helpful reference tool for converting common units of measurement in the kitchen. Here's a basic conversion chart to get you started:

Volume

1 gallon (gal) = 128 fluid ounces (fl oz)
1 quart (qt) = 32 fl oz
1 pint (pt) = 16 fl oz
1 cup (c) = 8 fl oz
1 fluid ounce (fl oz) = 2 tablespoons (tbsp)
1 tablespoon (tbsp) = 3 teaspoons (tsp)

CONVERSION CHART

1 gallon (gal) = 4 quarts (qt) = 8 pints (pt) = 128 fluid ounces (fl oz)

1 quart (qt) = 2 pints (pt) = 32 fluid ounces (fl oz)

1 pint (pt) = 16 fluid ounces (fl oz)

1 cup (c) = 8 fluid ounces (fl oz) = 16 tablespoons (tbsp) = 48 teaspoons (tsp)

1 fluid ounce (fl oz) = 2 tablespoons (tbsp) = 6 teaspoons (tsp)

CONVERSION CHART

Weight

1 pound (lb) = 16 ounces (oz)

1 ounce (oz) = 16 drams (dr)

1 gram (g) ≈ 0.0353 ounces (oz)

1 kilogram (kg) = 1,000 grams (g)

Temperature:

0°C (Celsius) = 32°F (Fahrenheit)

(freezing point of water)

100°C (Celsius) = 212°F (Fahrenheit)

(boiling point of water)

Length:

1 inch (in) = 2.54 centimeters (cm)

1 foot (ft) = 12 inches

1 yard (yd) = 3 feet

CONVERSION CHART

Common Ingredient Conversions:

1 cup (c) all-purpose flour = 120 grams (g)

1 cup (c) granulated sugar = 200 grams (g)

1 cup (c) butter (salted) = 227 grams (g)

1 cup (c) milk = 240 milliliters (mL)

1 tablespoon (tbsp) = 15 milliliters (mL)

1 teaspoon (tsp) = 5 milliliters (mL)

RECIPE JOURNAL

RECIPE NAME

COOKING TIME

INGREDIENTS

INSTRUCTIONS

-
-
-
-
-

COOKING TIPS AND NOTES

PERSONAL COMMENTS, RATINGS AND OBSERVATIONS

RECIPE JOURNAL

RECIPE NAME

COOKING TIME

....

....

INGREDIENTS

INSTRUCTIONS

- ....
- ....
- ....
- ....
- ....

....

....

....

COOKING TIPS AND NOTES

....

....

....

PERSONAL COMMENTS, RATINGS AND OBSERVATIONS

RECIPE JOURNAL

RECIPE NAME

COOKING TIME

....

....

INGREDIENTS

INSTRUCTIONS

- ....
- ....
- ....
- ....
- ....

....

....

....

COOKING TIPS AND NOTES

....

....

....

PERSONAL COMMENTS, RATINGS AND OBSERVATIONS

RECIPE JOURNAL

RECIPE NAME

COOKING TIME

....

....

INGREDIENTS

INSTRUCTIONS

- ....
- ....
- ....
- ....
- ....

....

....

....

....

COOKING TIPS AND NOTES

....

....

....

PERSONAL COMMENTS, RATINGS AND
OBSERVATIONS

RECIPE JOURNAL

RECIPE NAME

COOKING TIME

INGREDIENTS

INSTRUCTIONS

-
-
-
-
-

COOKING TIPS AND NOTES

PERSONAL COMMENTS, RATINGS AND OBSERVATIONS

RECIPE JOURNAL

RECIPE NAME

COOKING TIME

INGREDIENTS

INSTRUCTIONS

-
-
-
-
-

COOKING TIPS AND NOTES

PERSONAL COMMENTS, RATINGS AND OBSERVATIONS

RECIPE JOURNAL

RECIPE NAME

COOKING TIME

....

....

INGREDIENTS

INSTRUCTIONS

- ....
- ....
- ....
- ....
- ....

....

....

....

....

COOKING TIPS AND NOTES

....

....

....

PERSONAL COMMENTS, RATINGS AND OBSERVATIONS

RECIPE JOURNAL

RECIPE NAME

COOKING TIME

....

....

INGREDIENTS

INSTRUCTIONS

- ....
- ....
- ....
- ....
- ....

....

....

....

COOKING TIPS AND NOTES

....

....

....

PERSONAL COMMENTS, RATINGS AND OBSERVATIONS

RECIPE JOURNAL

RECIPE NAME

COOKING TIME

....

....

INGREDIENTS

INSTRUCTIONS

- ....
- ....
- ....
- ....
- ....

....

....

....

COOKING TIPS AND NOTES

....

....

....

PERSONAL COMMENTS, RATINGS AND OBSERVATIONS

RECIPE JOURNAL

RECIPE NAME

COOKING TIME

INGREDIENTS

INSTRUCTIONS

-
-
-
-
-

COOKING TIPS AND NOTES

PERSONAL COMMENTS, RATINGS AND
OBSERVATIONS

RECIPE JOURNAL

RECIPE NAME

COOKING TIME

....

....

INGREDIENTS

INSTRUCTIONS

- ....
- ....
- ....
- ....
- ....

....

....

COOKING TIPS AND NOTES

....

....

....

PERSONAL COMMENTS, RATINGS AND OBSERVATIONS

RECIPE JOURNAL

RECIPE NAME

COOKING TIME

....

....

INGREDIENTS

INSTRUCTIONS

- ....
- ....
- ....
- ....
- ....

....

....

....

....

COOKING TIPS AND NOTES

....

....

....

PERSONAL COMMENTS, RATINGS AND OBSERVATIONS

RECIPE JOURNAL

RECIPE NAME

COOKING TIME

....

....

INGREDIENTS

INSTRUCTIONS

- ....
- ....
- ....
- ....
- ....
  ....
  ....
  ....

COOKING TIPS AND NOTES

....

....

....

PERSONAL COMMENTS, RATINGS AND
OBSERVATIONS

RECIPE JOURNAL

RECIPE NAME

INSTRUCTIONS

- ....
- ....
- ....
- ....
- ....
....
....
....

COOKING TIME

....
....

INGREDIENTS

COOKING TIPS AND NOTES

....
....
....

PERSONAL COMMENTS, RATINGS AND
OBSERVATIONS

RECIPE JOURNAL

RECIPE NAME

COOKING TIME

....

....

INGREDIENTS

INSTRUCTIONS

- ....
- ....
- ....
- ....
- ....

....

....

....

COOKING TIPS AND NOTES

....

....

....

PERSONAL COMMENTS, RATINGS AND
OBSERVATIONS

RECIPE JOURNAL

RECIPE NAME

COOKING TIME

....

....

INGREDIENTS

INSTRUCTIONS

- ....
- ....
- ....
- ....
- ....

....

....

....

....

COOKING TIPS AND NOTES

....

....

....

PERSONAL COMMENTS, RATINGS AND OBSERVATIONS

RECIPE JOURNAL

RECIPE NAME

COOKING TIME

INGREDIENTS

INSTRUCTIONS

- ....
- ....
- ....
- ....
- ....

....

....

....

COOKING TIPS AND NOTES

....

....

....

PERSONAL COMMENTS, RATINGS AND OBSERVATIONS

RECIPE JOURNAL

RECIPE NAME

COOKING TIME

....

....

INGREDIENTS

INSTRUCTIONS

- ....
- ....
- ....
- ....
- ....

....

....

....

....

COOKING TIPS AND NOTES

....

....

....

PERSONAL COMMENTS, RATINGS AND
OBSERVATIONS

RECIPE JOURNAL

RECIPE NAME

COOKING TIME

INGREDIENTS

INSTRUCTIONS

- ....
- ....
- ....
- ....
-
  ....
  ....
  ....
  ....

COOKING TIPS AND NOTES

....
....
....

PERSONAL COMMENTS, RATINGS AND OBSERVATIONS

RECIPE JOURNAL

RECIPE NAME

COOKING TIME

....

....

INGREDIENTS

INSTRUCTIONS

- ....
- ....
- ....
- ....
- ....

....

....

....

....

COOKING TIPS AND NOTES

....

....

....

PERSONAL COMMENTS, RATINGS AND OBSERVATIONS

RECIPE JOURNAL

RECIPE NAME

COOKING TIME

....

....

INGREDIENTS

INSTRUCTIONS

- •
....
- •
....
- •
....
- •
....
- •
....

....

....

....

COOKING TIPS AND NOTES

....

....

....

PERSONAL COMMENTS, RATINGS AND OBSERVATIONS

RECIPE JOURNAL

RECIPE NAME

COOKING TIME

....

....

INGREDIENTS

INSTRUCTIONS

- ....
- ....
- ....
- ....
- ....

....

....

....

....

COOKING TIPS AND NOTES

....

....

....

PERSONAL COMMENTS, RATINGS AND OBSERVATIONS

RECIPE JOURNAL

RECIPE NAME

COOKING TIME

....

....

INGREDIENTS

INSTRUCTIONS

- ....
- ....
- ....
- ....
- ....

....

....

....

....

COOKING TIPS AND NOTES

....

....

....

PERSONAL COMMENTS, RATINGS AND OBSERVATIONS

RECIPE JOURNAL

RECIPE NAME

COOKING TIME

INGREDIENTS

INSTRUCTIONS

- ....
- ....
- ....
- ....
- ....
....
....
....
....

COOKING TIPS AND NOTES

....
....
....

PERSONAL COMMENTS, RATINGS AND OBSERVATIONS

RECIPE JOURNAL

RECIPE NAME

COOKING TIME

....

....

INGREDIENTS

INSTRUCTIONS

- ....
- ....
- ....
- ....
- ....
....
....
....
....

COOKING TIPS AND NOTES

....

....

....

PERSONAL COMMENTS, RATINGS AND OBSERVATIONS

RECIPE JOURNAL

RECIPE NAME

COOKING TIME

INGREDIENTS

INSTRUCTIONS

- ....
- ....
- ....
- ....
- ....

....

....

....

....

COOKING TIPS AND NOTES

....

....

....

PERSONAL COMMENTS, RATINGS AND OBSERVATIONS

RECIPE JOURNAL

RECIPE NAME

COOKING TIME

INGREDIENTS

INSTRUCTIONS

- ....
- ....
- ....
- ....
- ....
....
....
....

COOKING TIPS AND NOTES

....
....
....

PERSONAL COMMENTS, RATINGS AND OBSERVATIONS

RECIPE JOURNAL

RECIPE NAME

COOKING TIME

....

....

INGREDIENTS

INSTRUCTIONS

- ....
- ....
- ....
- ....
- ....

....

....

....

COOKING TIPS AND NOTES

....

....

....

PERSONAL COMMENTS, RATINGS AND
OBSERVATIONS

RECIPE JOURNAL

RECIPE NAME

COOKING TIME

....

....

INGREDIENTS

INSTRUCTIONS

- ....
- ....
- ....
- ....
- ....

....

....

....

COOKING TIPS AND NOTES

....

....

....

PERSONAL COMMENTS, RATINGS AND OBSERVATIONS

RECIPE JOURNAL

RECIPE NAME

COOKING TIME

INGREDIENTS

INSTRUCTIONS

-
-
-
-
-

COOKING TIPS AND NOTES

PERSONAL COMMENTS, RATINGS AND OBSERVATIONS

RECIPE JOURNAL

RECIPE NAME

COOKING TIME

....

....

INGREDIENTS

INSTRUCTIONS

- ....
- ....
- ....
- ....
- ....
....
....
....
....

COOKING TIPS AND NOTES

....

....

....

PERSONAL COMMENTS, RATINGS AND OBSERVATIONS

RECIPE JOURNAL

RECIPE NAME

COOKING TIME

....

....

INGREDIENTS

INSTRUCTIONS

- ....
- ....
- ....
- ....
- ....

....

....

....

COOKING TIPS AND NOTES

....

....

....

PERSONAL COMMENTS, RATINGS AND OBSERVATIONS

RECIPE JOURNAL

RECIPE NAME

COOKING TIME

INGREDIENTS

INSTRUCTIONS

- ....
- ....
- ....
- ....
- ....
....
....
....
....

COOKING TIPS AND NOTES

....
....
....

PERSONAL COMMENTS, RATINGS AND OBSERVATIONS

SHOPPING LIST AND RECIPE RATING

elcome to the heart of your culinary journey – the Shopping List
d Recipe Rating sections of your recipe workbook. These pages
ay a vital role in enhancing your cooking experience, making it
ore organized and enjoyable.

opping List: Your Recipe's Best Friend

our culinary adventure begins at the grocery store, and this
ction is here to help. Use the Shopping List to jot down the
gredients you need for your upcoming culinary creations.
hether it's a cozy family dinner or an elaborate feast, this section
sures that you're well-prepared, organized, and ready to bring
ur recipes to life.

p Tips for Using the Shopping List:

Plan Ahead: Before heading to the store, consult your recipes
d list the items you require.
Categorize:Group items by section (e.g., produce, dairy, pantry)
r efficient shopping.
Check Inventory:Note down essentials you may already have to
oid overbuying.
Add Personal Touch: Customize your shopping list with extra
ms or preferences for specific brands.

Recipe Rating: A Culinary Diary

The Recipe Rating section is where you get to be the food critic. After preparing and savoring your culinary creations, use this space to rate and review each recipe. Your ratings not only help you remember which dishes were your favorites but also offer valuable insights into your cooking skills and preferences.

Rating and Review Tips:

1. Taste: Rate the dish based on its flavor and your personal preferences.
2. Ease of Preparation:How easy or challenging was it to make?
3. Presentation: Did the dish look as appetizing as it tasted?
4. Personal Notes: Leave comments, suggestions, and ideas for improvements.

Remember, your shopping list and recipe ratings are not just practical tools; they are also a window into your culinary world. Let them guide you, inspire you, and reflect your evolving tastes and skills.

So, as you embark on your culinary adventures, let the Shopping List help you gather the ingredients, and the Recipe Rating section chronicl your delicious discoveries. Every dish you prepare is an opportunity to create a masterpiece, and your workbook is here to help you make the most of it.

Let's start filling those shopping lists and sharing your culinary critiques. Happy cooking!

Shopping List

DATE: / /

DAIRY:
- ○ _____
- ○ _____
- ○ _____
- ○ _____
- ○ _____
- ○ _____
- ○ _____
- ○ _____
- ○ _____
- ○ _____
- ○ _____
- ○ _____

MEAT & SEAFOOD:
- ○ _____
- ○ _____
- ○ _____
- ○ _____
- ○ _____
- ○ _____
- ○ _____
- ○ _____
- ○ _____
- ○ _____
- ○ _____

FRUITS & VEGGIES:
- ○ _____
- ○ _____
- ○ _____
- ○ _____
- ○ _____
- ○ _____
- ○ _____
- ○ _____

BREAD & CEREAL:
- ○ _____
- ○ _____
- ○ _____
- ○ _____
- ○ _____

OTHERS:
- ○ _____
- ○ _____
- ○ _____
- ○ _____
- ○ _____
- ○ _____
- ○ _____
- ○ _____
- ○ _____

FROZEN FOODS:
- ○ _____
- ○ _____
- ○ _____
- ○ _____
- ○ _____

CANNED GOODS:
- ○ _____
- ○ _____
- ○ _____
- ○ _____
- ○ _____

WHAT'S COOKING:
- S _____
- M _____
- T _____
- W _____
- T _____
- F _____
- S _____

DATE: / /

DAIRY:
○ _____
○ _____
○ _____
○ _____
○ _____
○ _____
○ _____
○ _____
○ _____
○ _____
○ _____
○ _____

MEAT & SEAFOOD:
○ _____
○ _____
○ _____
○ _____
○ _____
○ _____
○ _____
○ _____
○ _____
○ _____
○ _____
○ _____

FRUITS & VEGGIES:
○ _____
○ _____
○ _____
○ _____
○ _____
○ _____
○ _____
○ _____

BREAD & CEREAL:
○ _____
○ _____
○ _____
○ _____
○ _____

OTHERS:
○ _____
○ _____
○ _____
○ _____
○ _____
○ _____
○ _____
○ _____

FROZEN FOODS:
○ _____
○ _____
○ _____
○ _____
○ _____

CANNED GOODS:
○ _____
○ _____
○ _____
○ _____
○ _____

WHAT'S COOKING:
S _____
M _____
T _____
W _____
T _____
F _____
S _____

DATE: / /

DAIRY:
○ _____
○ _____
○ _____
○ _____
○ _____
○ _____
○ _____
○ _____
○ _____
○ _____
○ _____
○ _____

MEAT & SEAFOOD:
○ _____
○ _____
○ _____
○ _____
○ _____
○ _____
○ _____
○ _____
○ _____
○ _____
○ _____
○ _____

FRUITS & VEGGIES:
○ _____
○ _____
○ _____
○ _____
○ _____
○ _____
○ _____
○ _____

BREAD & CEREAL:
○ _____
○ _____
○ _____
○ _____
○ _____

OTHERS:
○ _____
○ _____
○ _____
○ _____
○ _____
○ _____
○ _____

FROZEN FOODS:
○ _____
○ _____
○ _____
○ _____
○ _____

CANNED GOODS:
○ _____
○ _____
○ _____
○ _____
○ _____

WHAT'S COOKING:
S _____
M _____
T _____
W _____
T _____
F _____
S _____

Shopping List

DATE: / /

DAIRY:
- ○ _____
- ○ _____
- ○ _____
- ○ _____
- ○ _____
- ○ _____
- ○ _____
- ○ _____
- ○ _____
- ○ _____
- ○ _____
- ○ _____

MEAT & SEAFOOD:
- ○ _____
- ○ _____
- ○ _____
- ○ _____
- ○ _____
- ○ _____
- ○ _____
- ○ _____
- ○ _____
- ○ _____
- ○ _____
- ○ _____

FRUITS & VEGGIES:
- ○ _____
- ○ _____
- ○ _____
- ○ _____
- ○ _____
- ○ _____
- ○ _____
- ○ _____

BREAD & CEREAL:
- ○ _____
- ○ _____
- ○ _____
- ○ _____
- ○ _____

OTHERS:
- ○ _____
- ○ _____
- ○ _____
- ○ _____
- ○ _____
- ○ _____
- ○ _____
- ○ _____

FROZEN FOODS:
- ○ _____
- ○ _____
- ○ _____
- ○ _____
- ○ _____

CANNED GOODS:
- ○ _____
- ○ _____
- ○ _____
- ○ _____
- ○ _____

WHAT'S COOKING:
- **S**
- **M**
- **T**
- **W**
- **T**
- **F**
- **S**

DATE: / /

DAIRY:
- ○ _____
- ○ _____
- ○ _____
- ○ _____
- ○ _____
- ○ _____
- ○ _____
- ○ _____
- ○ _____
- ○ _____
- ○ _____
- ○ _____

MEAT & SEAFOOD:
- ○ _____
- ○ _____
- ○ _____
- ○ _____
- ○ _____
- ○ _____
- ○ _____
- ○ _____
- ○ _____
- ○ _____
- ○ _____
- ○ _____

FRUITS & VEGGIES:
- ○ _____
- ○ _____
- ○ _____
- ○ _____
- ○ _____
- ○ _____
- ○ _____
- ○ _____

BREAD & CEREAL:
- ○ _____
- ○ _____
- ○ _____
- ○ _____
- ○ _____

OTHERS:
- ○ _____
- ○ _____
- ○ _____
- ○ _____
- ○ _____
- ○ _____
- ○ _____
- ○ _____

FROZEN FOODS:
- ○ _____
- ○ _____
- ○ _____
- ○ _____
- ○ _____

CANNED GOODS:
- ○ _____
- ○ _____
- ○ _____
- ○ _____
- ○ _____

WHAT'S COOKING:
- S _____
- M _____
- T _____
- W _____
- T _____
- F _____
- S _____

DATE: / /

DAIRY:
- ○ _____
- ○ _____
- ○ _____
- ○ _____
- ○ _____
- ○ _____
- ○ _____
- ○ _____
- ○ _____
- ○ _____
- ○ _____
- ○ _____

MEAT & SEAFOOD:
- ○ _____
- ○ _____
- ○ _____
- ○ _____
- ○ _____
- ○ _____
- ○ _____
- ○ _____
- ○ _____
- ○ _____
- ○ _____

FRUITS & VEGGIES:
- ○ _____
- ○ _____
- ○ _____
- ○ _____
- ○ _____
- ○ _____
- ○ _____
- ○ _____

BREAD & CEREAL:
- ○ _____
- ○ _____
- ○ _____
- ○ _____
- ○ _____

OTHERS:
- ○ _____
- ○ _____
- ○ _____
- ○ _____
- ○ _____
- ○ _____
- ○ _____
- ○ _____

FROZEN FOODS:
- ○ _____
- ○ _____
- ○ _____
- ○ _____
- ○ _____

CANNED GOODS:
- ○ _____
- ○ _____
- ○ _____
- ○ _____
- ○ _____

WHAT'S COOKING:
- S _____
- M _____
- T _____
- W _____
- T _____
- F _____
- S _____

DATE: / /

DAIRY:
○ _____
○ _____
○ _____
○ _____
○ _____
○ _____
○ _____
○ _____
○ _____
○ _____
○ _____
○ _____

FRUITS & VEGGIES:
○ _____
○ _____
○ _____
○ _____
○ _____
○ _____
○ _____
○ _____

BREAD & CEREAL:
○ _____
○ _____
○ _____
○ _____
○ _____

FROZEN FOODS:
○ _____
○ _____
○ _____
○ _____
○ _____

CANNED GOODS:
○ _____
○ _____
○ _____
○ _____
○ _____

MEAT & SEAFOOD:
○ _____
○ _____
○ _____
○ _____
○ _____
○ _____
○ _____
○ _____
○ _____
○ _____
○ _____

OTHERS:
○ _____
○ _____
○ _____
○ _____
○ _____
○ _____
○ _____

WHAT'S COOKING:
S _____
M _____
T _____
W _____
T _____
F _____
S _____

DATE: / /

DAIRY:
- ○ _____
- ○ _____
- ○ _____
- ○ _____
- ○ _____
- ○ _____
- ○ _____
- ○ _____
- ○ _____
- ○ _____
- ○ _____
- ○ _____

MEAT & SEAFOOD:
- ○ _____
- ○ _____
- ○ _____
- ○ _____
- ○ _____
- ○ _____
- ○ _____
- ○ _____
- ○ _____
- ○ _____
- ○ _____
- ○ _____

FRUITS & VEGGIES:
- ○ _____
- ○ _____
- ○ _____
- ○ _____
- ○ _____
- ○ _____
- ○ _____
- ○ _____

BREAD & CEREAL:
- ○ _____
- ○ _____
- ○ _____
- ○ _____
- ○ _____

OTHERS:
- ○ _____
- ○ _____
- ○ _____
- ○ _____
- ○ _____
- ○ _____
- ○ _____
- ○ _____

FROZEN FOODS:
- ○ _____
- ○ _____
- ○ _____
- ○ _____
- ○ _____

CANNED GOODS:
- ○ _____
- ○ _____
- ○ _____
- ○ _____
- ○ _____

WHAT'S COOKING:
- S _____
- M _____
- T _____
- W _____
- T _____
- F _____
- S _____

Shopping List

DATE: / /

DAIRY:
- ○ _____
- ○ _____
- ○ _____
- ○ _____
- ○ _____
- ○ _____
- ○ _____
- ○ _____
- ○ _____
- ○ _____
- ○ _____
- ○ _____

MEAT & SEAFOOD:
- ○ _____
- ○ _____
- ○ _____
- ○ _____
- ○ _____
- ○ _____
- ○ _____
- ○ _____
- ○ _____
- ○ _____
- ○ _____
- ○ _____

FRUITS & VEGGIES:
- ○ _____
- ○ _____
- ○ _____
- ○ _____
- ○ _____
- ○ _____
- ○ _____
- ○ _____

BREAD & CEREAL:
- ○ _____
- ○ _____
- ○ _____
- ○ _____
- ○ _____

OTHERS:
- ○ _____
- ○ _____
- ○ _____
- ○ _____
- ○ _____
- ○ _____
- ○ _____
- ○ _____

FROZEN FOODS:
- ○ _____
- ○ _____
- ○ _____
- ○ _____
- ○ _____

CANNED GOODS:
- ○ _____
- ○ _____
- ○ _____
- ○ _____
- ○ _____

WHAT'S COOKING:

- S
- M
- T
- W
- T
- F
- S

DATE: / /

DAIRY:
○ _____
○ _____
○ _____
○ _____
○ _____
○ _____
○ _____
○ _____
○ _____
○ _____
○ _____
○ _____

MEAT & SEAFOOD:
○ _____
○ _____
○ _____
○ _____
○ _____
○ _____
○ _____
○ _____
○ _____
○ _____
○ _____

FRUITS & VEGGIES:
○ _____
○ _____
○ _____
○ _____
○ _____
○ _____
○ _____
○ _____
○ _____

BREAD & CEREAL:
○ _____
○ _____
○ _____
○ _____
○ _____

OTHERS:
○ _____
○ _____
○ _____
○ _____
○ _____
○ _____
○ _____
○ _____

FROZEN FOODS:
○ _____
○ _____
○ _____
○ _____
○ _____

CANNED GOODS:
○ _____
○ _____
○ _____
○ _____
○ _____

WHAT'S COOKING:
S
M
T
W
T
F
S

DATE: / /

DAIRY:
○ _____
○ _____
○ _____
○ _____
○ _____
○ _____
○ _____
○ _____
○ _____
○ _____
○ _____
○ _____

MEAT & SEAFOOD:
○ _____
○ _____
○ _____
○ _____
○ _____
○ _____
○ _____
○ _____
○ _____
○ _____
○ _____
○ _____

FRUITS & VEGGIES:
○ _____
○ _____
○ _____
○ _____
○ _____
○ _____
○ _____
○ _____
○ _____

BREAD & CEREAL:
○ _____
○ _____
○ _____
○ _____
○ _____

OTHERS:
○ _____
○ _____
○ _____
○ _____
○ _____
○ _____
○ _____
○ _____
○ _____

FROZEN FOODS:
○ _____
○ _____
○ _____
○ _____
○ _____

CANNED GOODS:
○ _____
○ _____
○ _____
○ _____
○ _____

WHAT'S COOKING:
S
M
T
W
T
F
S

DATE: / /

DAIRY:
- ○ _____
- ○ _____
- ○ _____
- ○ _____
- ○ _____
- ○ _____
- ○ _____
- ○ _____
- ○ _____
- ○ _____
- ○ _____

FRUITS & VEGGIES:
- ○ _____
- ○ _____
- ○ _____
- ○ _____
- ○ _____
- ○ _____
- ○ _____
- ○ _____
- ○ _____

FROZEN FOODS:
- ○ _____
- ○ _____
- ○ _____
- ○ _____
- ○ _____

CANNED GOODS:
- ○ _____
- ○ _____
- ○ _____
- ○ _____
- ○ _____

BREAD & CEREAL:
- ○ _____
- ○ _____
- ○ _____
- ○ _____
- ○ _____

MEAT & SEAFOOD:
- ○ _____
- ○ _____
- ○ _____
- ○ _____
- ○ _____
- ○ _____
- ○ _____
- ○ _____
- ○ _____
- ○ _____
- ○ _____

OTHERS:
- ○ _____
- ○ _____
- ○ _____
- ○ _____
- ○ _____
- ○ _____
- ○ _____
- ○ _____

WHAT'S COOKING:
- **S** _____
- **M** _____
- **T** _____
- **W** _____
- **T** _____
- **F** _____
- **S** _____

DATE: / /

DAIRY:
○ _____
○ _____
○ _____
○ _____
○ _____
○ _____
○ _____
○ _____
○ _____
○ _____
○ _____
○ _____

FRUITS & VEGGIES:
○ _____
○ _____
○ _____
○ _____
○ _____
○ _____
○ _____
○ _____

FROZEN FOODS:
○ _____
○ _____
○ _____
○ _____
○ _____

CANNED GOODS:
○ _____
○ _____
○ _____
○ _____
○ _____

BREAD & CEREAL:
○ _____
○ _____
○ _____
○ _____
○ _____

MEAT & SEAFOOD:
○ _____
○ _____
○ _____
○ _____
○ _____
○ _____
○ _____
○ _____
○ _____
○ _____
○ _____

OTHERS:
○ _____
○ _____
○ _____
○ _____
○ _____
○ _____
○ _____
○ _____

WHAT'S COOKING:
S _____
M _____
T _____
W _____
T _____
F _____
S _____

Shopping List

DATE: / /

DAIRY:
- ○ _____
- ○ _____
- ○ _____
- ○ _____
- ○ _____
- ○ _____
- ○ _____
- ○ _____
- ○ _____
- ○ _____
- ○ _____
- ○ _____

MEAT & SEAFOOD:
- ○ _____
- ○ _____
- ○ _____
- ○ _____
- ○ _____
- ○ _____
- ○ _____
- ○ _____
- ○ _____
- ○ _____
- ○ _____
- ○ _____

FRUITS & VEGGIES:
- ○ _____
- ○ _____
- ○ _____
- ○ _____
- ○ _____
- ○ _____
- ○ _____
- ○ _____

BREAD & CEREAL:
- ○ _____
- ○ _____
- ○ _____
- ○ _____
- ○ _____

OTHERS:
- ○ _____
- ○ _____
- ○ _____
- ○ _____
- ○ _____
- ○ _____
- ○ _____
- ○ _____

FROZEN FOODS:
- ○ _____
- ○ _____
- ○ _____
- ○ _____
- ○ _____

CANNED GOODS:
- ○ _____
- ○ _____
- ○ _____
- ○ _____
- ○ _____

WHAT'S COOKING:
- S
- M
- T
- W
- T
- F
- S

Shopping List

DATE: / /

DAIRY:
○ _____
○ _____
○ _____
○ _____
○ _____
○ _____
○ _____
○ _____
○ _____
○ _____
○ _____
○ _____

MEAT & SEAFOOD:
○ _____
○ _____
○ _____
○ _____
○ _____
○ _____
○ _____
○ _____
○ _____
○ _____
○ _____
○ _____

FRUITS & VEGGIES:
○ _____
○ _____
○ _____
○ _____
○ _____
○ _____
○ _____
○ _____

BREAD & CEREAL:
○ _____
○ _____
○ _____
○ _____
○ _____

OTHERS:
○ _____
○ _____
○ _____
○ _____
○ _____
○ _____
○ _____
○ _____

FROZEN FOODS:
○ _____
○ _____
○ _____
○ _____
○ _____

CANNED GOODS:
○ _____
○ _____
○ _____
○ _____
○ _____

WHAT'S COOKING:
S
M
T
W
T
F
S

DATE: / /

DAIRY:
○ _____
○ _____
○ _____
○ _____
○ _____
○ _____
○ _____
○ _____
○ _____
○ _____
○ _____
○ _____

MEAT & SEAFOOD:
○ _____
○ _____
○ _____
○ _____
○ _____
○ _____
○ _____
○ _____
○ _____
○ _____
○ _____
○ _____

FRUITS & VEGGIES:
○ _____
○ _____
○ _____
○ _____
○ _____
○ _____
○ _____
○ _____

BREAD & CEREAL:
○ _____
○ _____
○ _____
○ _____
○ _____

OTHERS:
○ _____
○ _____
○ _____
○ _____
○ _____
○ _____
○ _____
○ _____

FROZEN FOODS:
○ _____
○ _____
○ _____
○ _____
○ _____

CANNED GOODS:
○ _____
○ _____
○ _____
○ _____
○ _____

WHAT'S COOKING:
S _____
M _____
T _____
W _____
T _____
F _____
S _____

Shopping List

DATE: / /

DAIRY:
- ○ _____
- ○ _____
- ○ _____
- ○ _____
- ○ _____
- ○ _____
- ○ _____
- ○ _____
- ○ _____
- ○ _____
- ○ _____
- ○ _____

MEAT & SEAFOOD:
- ○ _____
- ○ _____
- ○ _____
- ○ _____
- ○ _____
- ○ _____
- ○ _____
- ○ _____
- ○ _____
- ○ _____
- ○ _____
- ○ _____

FRUITS & VEGGIES:
- ○ _____
- ○ _____
- ○ _____
- ○ _____
- ○ _____
- ○ _____
- ○ _____
- ○ _____

BREAD & CEREAL:
- ○ _____
- ○ _____
- ○ _____
- ○ _____
- ○ _____

OTHERS:
- ○ _____
- ○ _____
- ○ _____
- ○ _____
- ○ _____
- ○ _____
- ○ _____
- ○ _____

FROZEN FOODS:
- ○ _____
- ○ _____
- ○ _____
- ○ _____
- ○ _____

CANNED GOODS:
- ○ _____
- ○ _____
- ○ _____
- ○ _____
- ○ _____

WHAT'S COOKING:
- S
- M
- T
- W
- T
- F
- S

DATE: / /

DAIRY:
○ _____
○ _____
○ _____
○ _____
○ _____
○ _____
○ _____
○ _____
○ _____
○ _____
○ _____
○ _____

MEAT & SEAFOOD:
○ _____
○ _____
○ _____
○ _____
○ _____
○ _____
○ _____
○ _____
○ _____
○ _____
○ _____
○ _____

FRUITS & VEGGIES:
○ _____
○ _____
○ _____
○ _____
○ _____
○ _____
○ _____
○ _____

BREAD & CEREAL:
○ _____
○ _____
○ _____
○ _____
○ _____

OTHERS:
○ _____
○ _____
○ _____
○ _____
○ _____
○ _____
○ _____
○ _____

FROZEN FOODS:
○ _____
○ _____
○ _____
○ _____
○ _____

CANNED GOODS:
○ _____
○ _____
○ _____
○ _____
○ _____

WHAT'S COOKING:
S
M
T
W
T
F
S

DATE: / /

DAIRY:
○ _____
○ _____
○ _____
○ _____
○ _____
○ _____
○ _____
○ _____
○ _____
○ _____
○ _____
○ _____

FRUITS & VEGGIES:
○ _____
○ _____
○ _____
○ _____
○ _____
○ _____
○ _____
○ _____

FROZEN FOODS:
○ _____
○ _____
○ _____
○ _____
○ _____

CANNED GOODS:
○ _____
○ _____
○ _____
○ _____
○ _____

BREAD & CEREAL:
○ _____
○ _____
○ _____
○ _____
○ _____

MEAT & SEAFOOD:
○ _____
○ _____
○ _____
○ _____
○ _____
○ _____
○ _____
○ _____
○ _____
○ _____
○ _____
○ _____

OTHERS:
○ _____
○ _____
○ _____
○ _____
○ _____
○ _____
○ _____
○ _____

WHAT'S COOKING:
S _____
M _____
T _____
W _____
T _____
F _____
S _____

Shopping List

DATE: / /

DAIRY:
- ○ _____
- ○ _____
- ○ _____
- ○ _____
- ○ _____
- ○ _____
- ○ _____
- ○ _____
- ○ _____
- ○ _____
- ○ _____
- ○ _____

MEAT & SEAFOOD:
- ○ _____
- ○ _____
- ○ _____
- ○ _____
- ○ _____
- ○ _____
- ○ _____
- ○ _____
- ○ _____
- ○ _____
- ○ _____
- ○ _____

FRUITS & VEGGIES:
- ○ _____
- ○ _____
- ○ _____
- ○ _____
- ○ _____
- ○ _____
- ○ _____
- ○ _____

BREAD & CEREAL:
- ○ _____
- ○ _____
- ○ _____
- ○ _____
- ○ _____

OTHERS:
- ○ _____
- ○ _____
- ○ _____
- ○ _____
- ○ _____
- ○ _____
- ○ _____
- ○ _____

FROZEN FOODS:
- ○ _____
- ○ _____
- ○ _____
- ○ _____
- ○ _____

CANNED GOODS:
- ○ _____
- ○ _____
- ○ _____
- ○ _____
- ○ _____

WHAT'S COOKING:
- **S** _____
- **M** _____
- **T** _____
- **W** _____
- **T** _____
- **F** _____
- **S** _____

DATE: /   /

DAIRY:
- ○ _____
- ○ _____
- ○ _____
- ○ _____
- ○ _____
- ○ _____
- ○ _____
- ○ _____
- ○ _____
- ○ _____
- ○ _____
- ○ _____

MEAT & SEAFOOD:
- ○ _____
- ○ _____
- ○ _____
- ○ _____
- ○ _____
- ○ _____
- ○ _____
- ○ _____
- ○ _____
- ○ _____
- ○ _____
- ○ _____

FRUITS & VEGGIES:
- ○ _____
- ○ _____
- ○ _____
- ○ _____
- ○ _____
- ○ _____
- ○ _____
- ○ _____

BREAD & CEREAL:
- ○ _____
- ○ _____
- ○ _____
- ○ _____
- ○ _____

OTHERS:
- ○ _____
- ○ _____
- ○ _____
- ○ _____
- ○ _____
- ○ _____
- ○ _____
- ○ _____

FROZEN FOODS:
- ○ _____
- ○ _____
- ○ _____
- ○ _____
- ○ _____

CANNED GOODS:
- ○ _____
- ○ _____
- ○ _____
- ○ _____
- ○ _____

WHAT'S COOKING:
- S
- M
- T
- W
- T
- F
- S

RECIPE RATING

Note:

RECIPE RATING

Note: _____

RECIPE RATING

Note:

RECIPE RATING

Note:

RECIPE RATING

Note: _____

RECIPE RATING

Note: _____

RECIPE RATING

Note:

RECIPE RATING

Note:

RECIPE RATING

Date:

RECIPE RATING

RECIPE RATING

Note:

RECIPE RATING

Note: _____

RECIPE RATING

Note:

RECIPE RATING

Note: _____

RECIPE RATING

Note:

RECIPE RATING

Note:

RECIPE RATING

Note:
_____

RECIPE RATING

Note: _____

Date: _____

RECIPE RATING

Note: _____

RECIPE RATING

NOTES

NOTES

NOTES

NOTES

NOTES

NOTES

Made in the USA
Las Vegas, NV
03 December 2024

13304874R00056